Rebecca Du

for **love** or **money**

A Christian Aid Lent course

Published by Christian Aid,
PO Box 100, London
SE1 7RT

ISBN number 0 904379 442

© Christian Aid 2000

Design: Visible Edge, London
Cover photo and centre page spread: Martin Parr/Magnum
Illustrations: Zoë Attwood

Contents

A transcript in Welsh is available to use alongside *For Love or Money* from Christian Aid, 27 Church Road, Whitchurch, Cardiff CF14 2DX. Tel: 029 2061 4435

Introduction

Why a course on money?

Money – getting, spending, owning, giving and wanting it – is one of the chief concerns of adult life. As things stand, important as money is to us, many of us have not explored its relationship with the other deepest values we profess. In fact, we can, as American Jesuit John Haughey writes, 'read the Gospel as if we have no money, and spend our money as if there was no Gospel'. If we believe that faith can shape every aspect of our lives, we may find that as our hearts and minds open to God's purposes, our wallets open too.

The five sessions in this course are designed to provide ways into these issues for groups and individuals; ways that are fun as well as searching and challenging. The sessions include Bible study, discussion, group exercises and personal reflection. We hope they will result in different ways of using money, and different ways of praying.

We have written each session to explore our actions about money in the light of what could be called a 'gospel twist'. For example:

- Getting: what kind of 'more' are we seeking?
- Spending: how do we hear God's call in the marketplace?
- Owning: money affects each of us; how does it affect all of us, as a community?
- Giving: what kind of giving is good news?
- Wanting: how do we make sense of all the things we desire?

We explore money and faith because we long for God's order and priorities to reign in us. We know from experience that recognising our heart's deepest desire – regardless of what it is – means that we want other things less. Jesus knew that too, as he gently reminded his disciples to seek the 'pearl of great price' (Matthew 13:45,46). In the pursuit of this treasure, he said, we find the Kingdom of Heaven. In all the talking, sharing and praying of this course we hope people will find ways to live more and more like that merchant, in pursuit of that pearl.

If we find it and choose it, our other wants and desires can find their proper place. There, in the words of 1 Timothy we will encounter 'the life that is really life'. Christian Aid has published this course because of the gospel witness that this life can transform all it touches; not just us, but all those with whom we share the world God loves so much.

This course is to help Christians:
• share insights in faith
• consider how faith changes the way we get, spend, own, give, and want money
• reflect on how money can change our worship and prayer life.

June 2000
Rebecca Dudley
Peter Graystone

Advice for group leaders

Your role

Money is, perhaps, the most practical subject anyone could choose for a Bible study. Your role as a leader on this course is to create the setting in which members of the group can make a connection between their faith and the way they live their lives day by day. This material invites them to do that by talking, thinking, writing, praying and taking part in activities together. It is group discussion material, not notes for you to base a long sermon on! So at times you should see yourself as the group's...

Organiser

There are some things the leader needs to think about so that the group doesn't have to – for instance, the layout of the chairs, the need for refreshments, the temperature of the room, lighting, the availability of equipment, and so on.

Host

Help the group feel at ease, especially if they do not initially know each other very well. Learn their names and introduce them to each other. Make friendly conversation before and after the meeting. Bear in mind things that people need to know in an unfamiliar setting, such as where the toilets are or whether it is acceptable to smoke indoors.

Timekeeper

The group will be relying on you to start and conclude the meeting at an agreed time. Timings are given in the book to help you. You need not be so rigid at adhering to them that a useful discussion gets cut off in its prime, but groups work best if everyone has confidence that the meetings will follow a consistent pattern.

Enabler

Make sure the group knows what is going to happen, when and why. Allow everyone to contribute if they wish to. That may mean gently asking one talkative person to hold back so that others can contribute, being aware of whether a quiet person wants to say something or prefers to listen, and even occasionally being a referee!

Encourager

The questions in this book do not have easy answers, but they are worth struggling with. They are not quiz questions with right or wrong answers. Rather, they are about sharing opinions and experiences. It is quite normal for discussion to go slowly at first. Don't be tempted to jump in with your own suggestions if there is a pause; people will warm up as they gain confidence in the group. Show that you value what members of the group say by looking at them while they are talking, listening to them and remembering what they say. It does not matter if the group cannot all agree before you move on to the next question; wrestling over something complex is of more value than accepting something bland.

Carer

Some things about money are favourite topics of conversation and laughter, but others are sensitive or personal. Your task is to make sure that the course is a positive experience for the group, being aware of feelings and sensing what is and isn't good to discuss. If painful emotions surface it is best not to try to pretend this isn't happening. Rather acknowledge it, commit it to God in prayer at some point during the meeting, and follow it up afterwards with a phone call or note. Meeting in a small group allows people to get to know and care for each other in a way that is not possible in the larger setting of a church service, so make the most of opportunities to support each other in Christian love.

Before the group meets

Our advice is to read through the whole book before you start the course so that you understand how it is set out and are unlikely to be taken by surprise. You will find that instructions to you, the group leader, are in italics. The rest of the text is directed at the group members. At various points there are stories or Bible passages which are conveyed best if one member of the group reads them aloud while others follow in their own copy of the book.

Make sure that everyone knows on what day the group will meet for the first time, where and when. This does not necessarily mean you making all the phone calls in person, but make sure there is a plan so that no one is left out.

There are some things which everybody will need for each meeting, so be sure you have worked out how they will be available. People can either be responsible for bringing their own or they can be provided at the first meeting, but be sure that it is clear which is the case. Other materials are needed for one session only, and it is simplest if the leader takes responsibility for providing those – you will find them listed at the beginning of each chapter. Each group member needs:
• a copy of this book
• a Bible.

Treat this book more like a tourist guide than the ten commandments! It is quite acceptable – indeed desirable – to adapt the material, leave some of it out, or introduce a better idea. You might do this because you find the suggestions take too long to get through them all, or because they do not ideally fit the social circumstances of the group, or simply because some ideas look more engaging than others. However, be sure to keep a balance between looking at the Bible, praying, and hearing about each others' points of view.

Based on the experience of groups that piloted the material before it was published, each session is timed to last 90 minutes. Obviously this is going to vary depending on the nature of the group. Participants who are well-known to each other will usually talk at greater length than new groups, who may need a variety of items introduced at a lively pace. One suggested approach is to meet for coffee, 30 minutes before the official starting time, followed by a prompt start and strictly timed finish. However, better suggestions may emerge if the group discusses these arrangements at their first meeting.

Moneybox

In ancient legend, Saint Benedict, riding from chapel one Sunday, met a peasant. 'You've got an easy job,' said the peasant. 'Why don't I become a man of prayer, then I could ride on horseback?' 'What makes you think praying is easy?' responded the monk. 'If you can say the Lord's Prayer just once without your attention wandering from the holy God, I'll give you the horse!' The astonished peasant leapt at the opportunity. 'Our Father, who art in heaven, hallowed be thy name, thy Kingdom come, thy...'. Suddenly he stopped and looked up at Benedict, 'Will you give me the saddle as well?'

Each week

Set aside the same time in your diary each week for preparation – not just the frantic half-hour before people arrive. Pray that God will help you grow personally through what you do and say together, and then pray for the rest of the group by name.

Recall the last time the group met.
- Did I talk too much?
- Did anyone get left out, or dominate?
- Is there a better way to 'break the ice'?
- Was there a good balance between talk and action, Bible study and prayer, reflection and chat?
- Was there any 'unfinished business'?

Read the chapter of this book that you are going to work through together. In particular, read the Bible passages making sure that you are really familiar with what the writer is saying. How is it relevant to your own life? Then...
- try to predict questions that might come up, knowing the group you have, and think how you will deal with them
- based on how previous weeks have gone, work out which parts you will leave out if time runs out
- if an extra idea occurs to you – a news story, a local example, a question from your own experience – scribble it in the margin
- check what equipment you require and gather it together
- think who would enjoy reading the various parts aloud and ask them in advance. Don't assume that everyone is comfortable with reading without preparation. Poor eyesight, shyness or reading ability might make a sudden request embarrassing to them.

On the night

Arrive at the venue early, or if it is in your own home prepare everything well in advance, so that when the doorbell rings you can give your attention to people rather than furniture. Depending on the circumstances, you might consider the following:
- how can the chairs be arranged so that everyone can see each other?
- what is needed concerning temperature, ventilation, comfort?
- will any of the group have special needs which can be prepared for to avoid embarrassment?
- where can dripping umbrellas be put?
- how will refreshments be served?
- should the phone be disconnected?

Tell God your thoughts about all of this. Then expect great things!

☼ Session 1 **Getting**

What kind of 'more' are we seeking?

Prepare   Bible text: Luke 12:13-21

The notes to the leader are written in italics; other comments are directed to group members.
- *Read the whole of this booklet, especially this chapter, the introduction and the advice for group leaders.*
- *Identify who will be in the group. Pray for its progress.*
- *Make sure there are copies of the booklet available for each group member to have one.*
- *Identify music to use for the opening reflections.*
  You can either:
  - *choose your own music*
  - *buy some suggested titles from Christian Aid's resource catalogue. Tick and send off the response form at the back of this booklet to order a free copy*
  - *learn and use the simple song on page 13 each week.*

In addition to a Bible and a copy of this book for each group member, for this session you will need:
- *a pencil or pen for everyone*
- *recorded music to aid reflection (optional).*

Identify people in advance to prepare to read:
- *the opening and closing prayers*
- *the Bible reading.*

Gather   Introduction (10 minutes)
In a new group, invite everyone to introduce himself or herself by name and church, if appropriate. Explain that:
- *this is a five session course, and the group will benefit if everyone can come to all sessions*
- *participation is invited but optional in every activity*
- *you will not always reach agreement. Aim for new insights from each other, and to bring unresolved difficulties to prayer*
- *what is shared in the group is confidential.*

Ask what pattern the group would like to follow for meetings, how and when they would like to take refreshments, and confirm what time the meeting will start and finish.

Money is a very practical subject for Bible study, so it is possible that you may find the way you think, and what you do, changing as a result of what you discover on this course. At this point, the very beginning of the course, think back to a memory you have of money from a long time ago, and tell the others. It could be about:
• the pocket money you had when you were young, and how you spent it
• your very first wage packet
• the coins from your youth which have changed through the years.

As you hear members of the course share their stories, reflect on what you hope this course might achieve for you as an individual and for your group.

When everyone who wishes to has had a chance to introduce themselves with a memory in this way, look at the authors' hopes for the course, which conclude the introduction on page 5.

Is there anything you would like to add about your personal hopes for the course? It may not be possible to meet all these goals, but hearing them may help guide the group and the leader.

Opening prayers (5 minutes)
Read the following introduction slowly and allow a little time for people to relax.

Leader   Sit comfortably with your back supported,,, your feet on the floor... your shoulders relaxed... become aware of your breathing, in and out.

Think about the activities of the day that you have left behind to be here... and now turn your thoughts to this meeting, perhaps the last phase of your day.

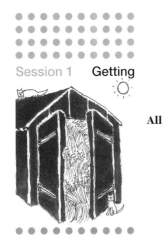

We pray together:

All   **Holy Spirit we invite you here among us
as we meet to nourish and challenge our faith,
so that our faith nourishes and challenges us
for our life in the world.
Help us to think and pray
in our getting and spending.
Bring your order to our owning.
Guide our giving.
And provoke in us the desire above all
to see your kingdom here on earth as it is in heaven.**

Keep silence

Invite someone to lead the following prayer.

Reader My soul's desire is to see the face of God,
All   **and to rest in his house.**
Reader My soul's desire is to study the scriptures,
All   **and to see the face of God.**
Reader My soul's desire is to be freed from all fear and sadness,
All   **and to share Christ's risen life.**
Reader My soul's desire is to enter the gates of heaven,
All   **and to gaze upon the light that shines for ever.
Dear Lord: you alone know what my soul truly desires,
and you alone can satisfy those desires. Amen.**

(Celtic Fire, Robert Van de Meyer, ed., Longman and Todd, London, 1990 p95)

*Sing together the song 'Take, O take me as I am' which may be
found on page 13.*

*Alternatively, play about two minutes of music that is suitable
for setting a mood of reflection. Any music that suggests
stillness or peace of God is suitable, either live or recorded.*

Reflect Thinking back (10 minutes)
This activity is for group members to work on by themselves.

We are about to read a parable of Jesus, in which a man has
a conversation with his soul. So let us prepare for having a
quick word with our souls!

Take, O take me as I am

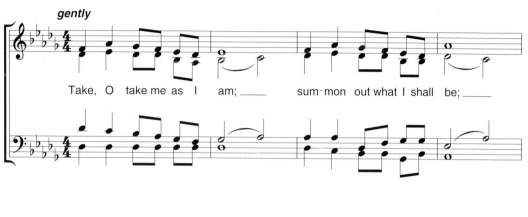

Take, O take me as I am; _____ sum-mon out what I shall be; _____

set your seal up - on my heart and live in me. _____

Take, O take me as I am;
summon out what I shall be;
set your seal upon my heart
and live in me.

from 'Come All You People'
(Wild Goose Publications, 1995)
© 1995 WGRG, Iona Community
840 Govan Road, Glasgow G51 3UU
Scotland

Moneybox

● ● ● ● ● ● ● ● ● ●

We need to give
ourselves seven years
to let go of everything
that is indispensable –
beginning with what we
spend on prestige.

Taizé community papers:
'Creating a Money Autobiography'

In the first barn:

Write words, draw pictures, or make symbols to show some of the things that you are glad you have. You might include things you own or keep in your home, but you could also think of things that money cannot buy, ie health, family, a job.

In the second barn:

Write words, draw pictures, or make symbols to show some of the things that you want more of. This could range from 'world peace' to 'a new VCR'; but try to name what you actually spend time thinking about getting, rather than what you feel you should spend time on!

You will return to the third barn later!

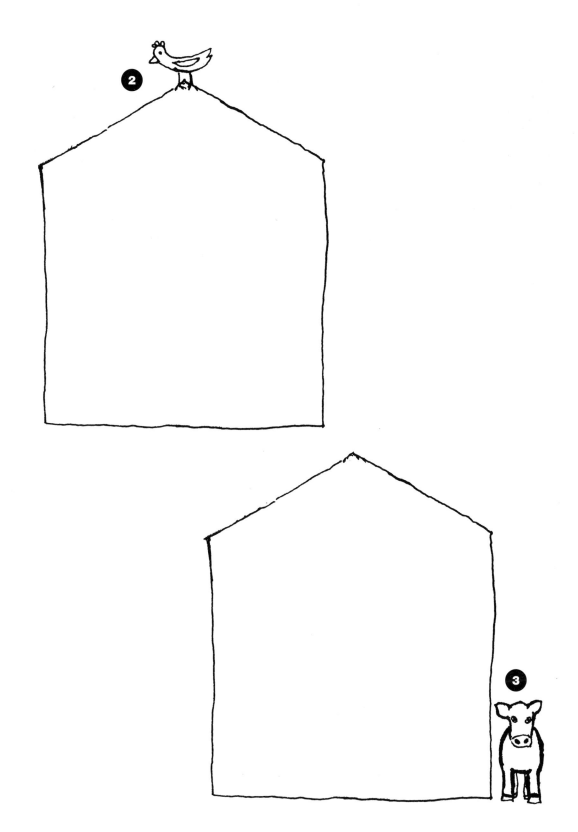

15

Bible reading (5 minutes)

Invite someone to read Luke 12:13-21.

Discussion (25 minutes)

- Look at what you have written or drawn in the barns. Comparing that with what you have just heard from the Bible, what strikes you first about the Bible text?
- Can you name any ways in which you can identify with:
  - the man in the parable?
  - the man who is asking about the inheritance?
  - the character of Jesus that this passage reveals?
- We know what the man in the parable said to his soul, thinking that he had time ahead to see his barns expand. What do you think he would have said to his soul if he knew he was going to die?
- What are the signs by which you and those around you could tell that you have:
  - enough money?
  - too much money?
- What does it mean to 'be rich towards God'? Try to consider what it might mean both from a 'spiritual' point of view and a 'material' one.

Thinking ahead (5 minutes)

Now for the third barn. In silence, write words, draw pictures, or make symbols to show what you could pursue to be what Jesus described as 'rich towards God'. You might use some of the items you have already put in the first or second barns, or add new ones – either solid possessions or things that money cannot buy.

What would Jesus say? (15 minutes)

Split the group into pairs so that there are several conversations going on at once. Allocate one of the statements below to each pair and ask them to consider the question.

In pairs, consider one of the statements below. Suppose the speaker stood in front of Jesus like the man in the Bible story did. What might Jesus say to him or her?

- Greed is good. Roll the words around your tongue...
  Greed is back in fashion.

'Greed is good again' *Guardian Finance*, 26 Feb 2000, p31

16

• Power has passed out of the hands of countries into the all-encompassing power of money. Money rules the world. Even the United States has possibly already passed its days of supremacy, since we may question whether America rules the dollar or the dollar rules America.

John Hull, *Mission, Education and Globalisation,* extracts from a sermon

• They love me in Japan. But unfortunately I don't want their love. I want their money.

Hugh Grant, Actor

• Life is so much better than it was in the past. But the cost of living is increasing. I can't really manage to buy the things I need for the household.

Olivia Tsuro, who leads a project to make money from baking and needlework, sponsored by Christian Aid, Makokaba Township, Zimbabwe

• Fifty per cent of you binge when you are feeling down; forty-two per cent go shopping... Retail therapy doesn't last long, because the lack always reinstates itself. The good news is that as the void we are filling will never be filled, we might as well keep shopping.

She magazine, April 2000, pp103, Linda Grant, *Vogue,* April 2000, p240

• In this little country everything is far away: food, learning, clothes.

Humberto Ak'abal, about the Central American country Guatemala, trans. Alex Linkater, *Guatemala: the right to dream,* eds Cynthia Kee and Reggie Norton, Asse of Artists for Guatemala, 1995

When everyone has finished talking to their partners, read the statements one at a time and, after each, invite people to share what they thought Jesus would say.

Looking ahead (5 minutes)

Now, by yourself, look back at the 'barns' you have filled.
• Identify, by ticking or circling, the areas in the barns where most of your money goes.
• Identify the areas you spend the least on.
• How does your use of money express your deepest values?

Imagine yourself now, in front of Jesus. What might Jesus be saying to you?

Moveybox

The Greek word in this passage (*ploenexia*) can be understood as 'a passion for more... an insatiability [greed] for more of what I already experience or have. If I had just a little bit more, I would be happy... I would be financially secure; I would not have this gnawing uncertainty – if I just had a little bit more.'
Avoid *ploenexia* in all its forms.
(Luke 12:15)

... When most of its people are incited to *ploenexia*... you have a culture that is propelled by insatiability.

John C. Haughey SJ, *Virtue and Affluence, the Challenge of Wealth,* chapter 4, A Passion for More, p19

As you reflect on the barns, and as in the Bible story, is there anything that you would like to say to your soul?
Write it in the box.

Soul...

Moneybox

The accumulation of wealth can only be justified if it is motivated by the need to fulfil specific obligations or anticipated future needs (eg saving up for necessary purchases rather than borrowing). Merely saving to achieve ever-greater levels of financial security equates to the worship of money.

Paul Mills, *Faith Versus Prudence: Christians and Financial Security,* Cambridge Papers *Towards a Biblical Mind,* Volume 4, number 1, March 1995, p4

After some moments for reflection, invite the group to share anything they wish.

Respond   **During the week** (5 minutes)

Look back at the third barn you filled. Identify one of the items you have put in the third barn to pursue this week. As this chapter is about 'getting', identify one thing you might do to 'get' that kind of wealth. This kind of wealth may have to do with silent, reflective insights into your faith and to active development of relationships of love and service.

Share your commitment with the person you were talking with earlier.

Closing reflection and prayer (5 minutes)
Invite two people to read the following prayers.

Reader 1   Then Jesus told his disciples, 'If any want to become my followers, let them deny themselves and take up their cross and follow me. For those who want to save their life will lose it, and those who lose their life for my sake will find it. For what will it profit them if they gain the whole world but forfeit their life?

(Matthew 16:24-26)

Reader 2   **The value of money**
With money, we can buy:
a bed, but no dreams;
books, but not intelligence;
food, but not appetite;
adornments, but not beauty;
a house, but not a home;
medicines, but not health;
children, but not joy;
entertainment, but not fun;
a crucifix, but not a Saviour;
a church, but not heaven.

Seen on the wall of a restaurant in Guatemala:
trans. Judith Escribano

Leader   We pray, as Jesus taught us:

All   **Our Father, who art in heaven,**
hallowed be thy name,
thy kingdom come,
thy will be done
on earth as it is in heaven.
Give us this day our daily bread,
forgive us our trespasses,
as we forgive those who trespass against us.
Lead us not into temptation,
but deliver us from evil.
For thine is the kingdom,
the power and the glory,
for ever and ever. Amen.

Moneybox
● ● ● ● ● ● ● ● ● ● ●

There is no need to be the richest man in the cemetery. You can't do business there.

Colonel Sanders, founder of the vast multi-national Kentucky Fried Chicken chain.

How do we hear God's call in the marketplace?

Prepare Bible texts: Isaiah 55:1-9; Matthew 6:19-21

In addition to a Bible and a copy of this book for each group member, for this session you will need:
- *two large sheets of paper headed 'Like' and 'Dislike'*
- *a felt marker*
- *fairly traded chocolate guaranteed with the Fairtrade Mark – see pages 22 and 27*
- *recorded music to aid reflection (optional).*

Identify people in advance to prepare to read:
- *the opening and closing prayers*
- *the two Bible readings*
- *the parts of José and the journalist in the story of the cocoa farmer.*

Gather **Introduction** (10 minutes)

If the group is meeting together for only the second time, everyone should have a chance to remind each other of their names and the church they come from.

Starting with the leader, everyone should say one thing they enjoy spending money on, and one way in which spending money is a negative experience. For example, someone might suggest shopping for Christmas presents as an enjoyable activity and putting petrol in the car as a miserable one – or of course, precisely the opposite might be the case! The leader should list the suggestions on two pieces of paper headed 'Likes' and 'Dislikes'. When everyone has had a turn, look at the lists. Do they reveal anything about you as a group?

Look back on last week's session, which finished with a suggestion of pursuing one idea about what it might mean to be 'rich toward God'. Have thoughts occurred or experiences happened during the week that would be valuable to share with the rest of the group?

Moneybox

A righteous man cares for the needs of his animal, but the kindest acts of the wicked are cruel.

Proverbs 12:10

Whatever would the writer of Proverbs have made of a battery hen coop?

20

Opening prayers (10 minutes)

Read the following introduction slowly and allow a little time for relaxation.

Leader   Let me invite you, just as I did last week, to sit comfortably with your back supported... your feet on the floor... your shoulders relaxed... becoming aware of your breathing, in and out.

Think about the lists we have made about what we like and dislike spending money on. In your imagination, think of the receipts you have received for things you have spent money on during this week... large purchase or small, each one represented on small slips of paper.

Clench your fists tightly as though you were hanging on to them. In the silence, tell God what you think about the purchases you made. Ask him to help you, during the course of this meeting, to see them in the way he sees them. As you speak to God in the quiet, unclench your fists slowly as a sign of handing over to him your thoughts about spending. Now the receipts rest in your open palms, waiting expectantly for God to speak to you today about the way in which you spend money, so that what you do in future may be more pleasing to him.

Keep silence

Invite the group to say the prayer on the inside front cover.

Reader   Lord Jesus Christ,
           so that I may buy only what is valuable,
All   **teach me to want only what is good.**
Reader   So that I may treat God in a rich way,
All   **teach me to treat riches in a godly way.**
Reader   So that I may cling tightly to God,
All   **teach me to cling lightly to what I purchase, until my soul is content in you. Amen.**

Sing the song on page 13 or play a piece of reflective music (optional).

Moneybox

● ● ● ● ● ● ● ● ●

He who works his land will have abundant food, but he who chases fantasies lacks judgment.

Proverbs 12:11

Never likely to become the motto of the advertising industry!

Session 2 Spending

Reflect

Bible reading (5 minutes)

Imagine that you are shopping in a market place like the one in EastEnders, or if you have a vivid imagination, one in the Middle East 500 years before Jesus. Try to picture the bustle and hear the voices of the stall keepers persuading you to stop and look at their wares. While you have that scene in your mind, listen to someone read Isaiah 55:1-9, which uses the language of street vendors to 'sell' something completely different!

Invite someone to read Isaiah 55:1-9.

Discussion (25 minutes)

- Pick out three or four things mentioned in the passage which can still be bought with money – things which offer life and nourishment, joy and health.
- The writer also talks about things that people spend money on, but which are not ultimately satisfying. What do you think he had in mind?
- Have you noticed differences between the way shopping takes place nowadays, and the way it did when you were young? Make a list of the changes you identify. Allow yourselves a few minutes of nostalgia before going on to discuss: have the changes had an impact in any way on our spiritual or inner lives, as individuals or as a nation? For instance: is it a coincidence that shopping arcades seem to look like temples? Can you think of advertisements that persuade us that purchasing something will increase our happiness? In what way do you think these changes have been good, and in what way do they bring dangers?
- The end of the passage tells us that the Lord's ways are higher than our ways. Does this mean that God is too holy to take an interest in the way we spend money? If not, what does it mean?
- Should 'seeking the Lord while he may be found' change the way we spend money? Is it ever right to buy something luxurious or frivolous? What questions should we ask before we purchase something? 'Can I afford it?' is an obvious one – but are there others?

Story from the Dominican Republic (20 minutes)

Place a bar of chocolate on a table in the middle of the group. The chocolate should ideally be a fairly traded product guaranteed with the Fairtrade mark. Read this introduction, and ask two people who enjoy reading to play the parts of José and the journalist as the story below is read.

Moveybox

The Lord detests differing weights, and dishonest scales do not please him.

Proverbs 20:10

Short shrift for the car salesman who turns back a mileometer!

In the middle of this booklet you will find some colour photographs. Two of them show José Rodriguez from the Dominican Republic. He is a farmer, growing cocoa beans. On the table you can see the end product of his work, which can be bought in this country. We do not always make the connection between the food we enjoy eating here and the circumstances which have brought it to our shop shelves. As you look at the picture and the chocolate bar, see if you can imagine the scene as we find out how he spends his days.

Journalist   We are in the Dominican Republic at the local headquarters of Conacado, a federation of cocoa farmers. The heat is intense and the air is still in the brightly-painted building. Spanish voices ricochet off the breeze-block walls, and we follow them into the warehouse. A man is sitting on a stool while the paperwork is processed on his sack of cocoa beans. He looks exhausted, and that is no surprise since he has just carried his precious harvest of beans 4km from his farm. The sack weighs 47kg, which is a heavy weight for anyone in a tropical climate. However, hiring a donkey leaves less money to live on, so you rely on your shoulders and a little help from local children. Even if, like this man, you are 81 years old.

We are here to meet José Rodriguez, who is a board member of Conacado, which has brought the farmers together to process, market and transport their crops. This allows them to get the best deal from the sale of their produce. Cocoa that comes from the federation makes the kind of chocolate that we buy in this country with a Fairtrade mark on it. This is chocolate that we can purchase in confidence that the workers who produced it have not been forced to accept an unfair price or work in dangerous conditions.

José   The local dealers used to treat us badly and earn a lot of money at our expense. Through the federation, and by improving the quality of the beans, it was possible to get more benefits. After so many years of bad experiences, we do not want to be treated badly any more.

Journalist   Still working daily at the age of 74, he speaks with great pride of his children and grandchildren.

José   I am a *bruto**.
I can barely sign my own name. I can count, but I know absolutely nothing.

*roughly translated as a 'rough diamond'

Moneybox

●●●●●●●●●●●

Food gained by fraud tastes sweet to a man, but he ends up with a mouth full of gravel.

Proverbs 20:17

Bad news for the house purchaser who takes advantage of a seller's difficulty to reduce their offer to lower than the true value.

23

Journalist   However, his four sons and a daughter all went to primary school, and some of his grandchildren have been able to go on to secondary education. One is training to be a priest.

José   The grandchildren are very intelligent. They try to improve themselves. I would wish many, many things for the future. Every day you want to improve more and more.

Journalist   This afternoon will find José back in the fields, because working the land is his only source of income.

José   I like working hard. Although at my age the arthritis does come into the bones... My life is not easy. I am not a person in search of money. I want that everybody has the means to have a decent life. Not only in this country, but everywhere people want to live in dignity. Everyone should have the possibility to live, to develop and to produce. I am not ambitious. I like to share what I have with everybody.

José Rodriguez was interviewed in Bonao, Dominican Republic, in 1999 by a journalist working with the Fairtrade Foundation.

Contact: the Fairtrade Foundation, Suite 204, 16 Baldwin's Gardens, London EC1N 7RJ

www.fairtrade.org.uk

In Ireland: Fairtrade Mark Ireland, Carmichael Centre, North Brunswick Street, Dublin 7

www.fair-mark.org

After listening to the story, discuss these questions:
• What strikes you about this story of how chocolate comes to us?
• What do we have that José lacks? What has he got that we don't have? Don't restrict your answers to material things!
• What are the arguments for and against buying fairly traded products?
• Look back at the first few verses of Isaiah 55. Do they seem relevant in any way to José's story or our response to it?

Respond   **During the week** (10 minutes)
Suggest to the group that they might like to do this activity during the week, and come next week with some thoughts about it.

Identify a few purchases this week. You may choose them because they are significant, or because they are very ordinary – part of your weekly grocery shop. Make a point of noting where these come from in the space on page 33, at the end of the section of colour photographs. This will be easy when you

Moneybox

'It's no good, it's no good!' says the buyer; then off he goes and boasts about his purchase.

Proverbs 20:14

Imagine a shopper who makes a false complaint about a leather jacket to get it at a reduced price, then crows to all his friends, 'What a bargain! Only £50, and the shop assistant was too dim to notice he was being fooled!'

shop for food or clothes, because the country of origin will be on the label. But try also to think of the international implications of other things you buy – travel, heat and light, insurance, entertainment, investments, etc. Here are some questions to help you think through the way you spend during this week.

- Is this purchase **Selfish**, or made with the needs of others in mind?
- Has this been an **Honest** purchase – for both seller and buyer?
- Is there anything **Oppressive** about this – will people or animals be harmed by it?
- Have I been **Persuaded** into something that will prevent me using the money in another way?

Selfish, **H**onest, **O**ppressive, **P**ersuaded. **SHOP**. That's quite a memorable acronym! If it comes to mind as you make a purchase this week, use the space to also write down the thoughts that occur to you.

Moneybox

● ● ● ● ● ● ● ● ● ●

An inheritance quickly gained at the beginning will not be blessed at the end.

Proverbs 20:21

What if this appeared on a sign next to the queue for lottery tickets!

Moneybox

● ● ● ● ● ● ● ● ● ● ●

A generous man will prosper; he who refreshes others will himself be refreshed. People curse the man who hoards grain, but blessing crowns him who is willing to sell.

Proverbs 11:25,26

How are the multinational companies who have so much power over the living standards of the world's poorest workers like the farmer who used to stockpile corn hoping for huge profits during the winter shortages?

Closing prayers (10 minutes)

In each of these intercessions, leave time during which members of the groups may spontaneously mention a name, a group or a country that comes to mind. Invite someone to read the following prayers.

Reader   Gracious God, we pray for all who work in shops, or who are involved in selling by telephone or on the Internet. Here we lift before you those people whom we know are connected in any way with shops.

During this time, members of the group may say aloud names of people known to them. After a short while continue.

Reader   We pray that they may have encouragement when they are tired, patience when customers or employers are difficult, and honesty in all circumstances.

And we pray for those who supply the products we buy from around the world. Here we lift before you workers in the countries that we know supply the raw materials for the products we enjoy.

During this time, members of the group may say the names of nations from which foods, textiles and minerals come.

Reader   Especially we pray for justice where a fair wage is denied, and safety where it is hazardous to bring us what we want to buy.

Lastly we pray for us all as we spend our money. Here we lift before you the names of the shops that we use.

During this time, mention shops and other contexts where money is spent.

Reader   Make us strong when marketing encourages us to be greedy, make us generous when habit encourages us to be selfish, and make us wise when it is not clear whether or not to buy.

Invite someone to read Matthew 6:19-21.

After spending a moment to reflect on the words of Jesus, invite someone to read this prayer.

Reader   Lord God, be with us every day of this week:
helping us to choose carefully,
helping us to spend wisely,
helping us to decide thoughtfully.
And so may every purchase we make
be done as if it was a gift to you. Amen.

*Close your prayers by saying the Lord's Prayer together
(the words in full are on page 19).*

Our Father...

*Close by sharing different kinds of chocolate, making sure to
include at least one that has been fairly traded (such as Divine
chocolate guaranteed with the Fairtrade Mark. Divine
chocolate and Green & Black's Maya Gold and milk chocolates
are available in many major supermarkets). Have a 'blind
tasting' to investigate whether it is possible to guess which
chocolate gave a fair wage and decent conditions to the people
who grew it!*

Olaf Tamm/Food Illustrated Magazine/Fairtrade Foundation

Previous page:
A market stall at the Dingle Races in the Republic of Ireland, for use during session 5

Right: Photographs of José Rodriguez, on his plantation in the Dominican Republic for use during session 2

Olaf Tamm/Food Illustrated Magazine/Fairtrade Foundation

Olaf Tamm/Food Illustrated Magazine/Fairtrade Foundation

Above: José Rodriguez

Above: Cocoa pods containing cocoa beans

Above: Cocoa beans drying in the sun

Above: The plantation in Bahia, where Maria works, for use during session 4

Which countries do this week's
purchases come from?

Selfish?
Honest?
Oppressive?
Persuaded?

Session 3 Owning

Money affects each of us; how does it affect all of us, as a community?

Prepare Bible text: James 2:1-7

In addition to a Bible and a copy of this book for each group member, for this session you will need:
- *credit card-sized cards for each member of the group (cut index cards in half)*
- *a pencil or pen for everyone*
- *a calculator*
- *recorded music to aid reflection (optional).*

Identify people in advance to prepare to read:
- *the opening and closing prayers*
- *the Bible reading*
- *four quotations from around the world.*

Gather Introduction (10 minutes)
Repeat the exercise which helps the group to settle, relax and focus on God as described at the beginning of the first session.

Invite the group to share experiences of using the SHOP acronym during the week.

Leader We have started opening our hearts and minds to God about the relationships between our faith and money. This week we will start our reflection by opening our wallets and purses as well. I would like to invite you to take out your wallet or purse, and empty the contents into your lap (eg for purses, the part where cards, photos, money, etc would be kept).

Invite group members to consider the following questions in silence.
- What do the contents of your wallet or purse show about something that you enjoy doing?
- What do the contents of your wallet or purse show about relationships that are important to you?
- How, if at all, do the contents of your wallet or purse affirm something you value deeply? Pause to acknowledge this to yourself.
- How, if at all, do the contents of your wallet or purse sit uneasily with your faith?

Moneybox

The richest 200 people in the world – 196 of them billionaires – have a net worth of $1,032 billion, the equivalent of the income of 41 per cent of the world's population.

The Guardian, 14 July 1999

After a silence, sing the song on page 13 or play a piece of reflective music (optional).

Opening prayers (5 minutes)
Invite the group to say the prayer on the inside front cover.

Encourage people to share comments about thinking and praying with their wallets open.

Reflect **Our standpoint in an unequal world** (20 minutes)
Although money is a very private matter, it is not only a private matter. We turn in this session to how money, or the lack of it, can affect everyone in the community.

American Jesuit John Haughey has observed that 'we read the Gospel as if we had no money, and spend our money as if there was no Gospel'. To confront this challenge, we have looked at spending our money over the last week. Now we prepare to read scriptures by considering where we stand financially, in relation to a wider community.

Moneybox

● ● ● ● ● ● ● ● ● ●

The top one per cent of earners has seen their incomes double since 1979, and whereas the chief executive of a US company could expect to earn 35 times as much as the average worker in 1973, today they will be coining in 200 times as much.

The Guardian, 14 July 1999

Below are some rough guides to how rich or poor we are in relation to others, people who might be outside our immediate experience – whether family and friends or what we see on TV and in magazines. These figures have some limitations, but as they deal with about six billion people, the result will not be far off!

The world community
Consider the table below. Each of the three columns represents over a billion people and their incomes. Tick the column that represents your income.

To give an idea of what this income level means, some examples have been sketched out about what food, transport and material goods people in this income level might use.

	Poorest	Middle income	Wealthy
Number of people	1.1 billion	3.3 billion	1.1 billion
Annual income per family member (1992)	under £450 ($700)	between £450-£5,000 ($700-$7,500)	more than £5,000 ($7,500)
Transport	walking	bicycles and public transport	private cars
Food	grain (but not enough) and unsafe water	grain and clean water	includes meat, processed foods, soft drinks
Material goods	products made from the local environment	long lasting manufactured products	disposable products

(Adapted from *'Distribution of People and Resources, The Southern Perspectives on Development Series,* written by Linnea Renton, Development Education Project, c/o The Manchester Metropolitan University, 801 Wilmslow Road, Didsbury, Manchester, M20 2QR, p15)

Invite brief discussion or comment.

The United Kingdom

There is, however, substantial and painful inequality within wealthy countries. Below is a table from 1996-97 (the latest available at the time of writing).

In this table, the population of Britain has been divided into five equal parts.

The top fifth is the 20 per cent of households with the highest incomes.

The bottom fifth is the 20 per cent of households with the lowest incomes.

Take these as a rough guide: for example, clergy and others may get housing benefits in addition. Others may have cars that go with their jobs, etc. To estimate the nearest category in which you fall:

- take your net household yearly income
  (eg after taxes, benefits)
- add £2,000 per person in your household (because the statistics office say that is what the National Health Service benefit is worth to each of us, on average)
- tick that column.

	Bottom fifth	Next fifth	Middle fifth	Next fifth	Top fifth	National average for all households
Final income average per household [1]	£8,310	£10,600	£14,490	£19,040	£31,790	£16,850

(1) After taxes, and adjusting for other kinds of income: benefits (in cash and in kind, like the NHS), self employed income, pensions, investments, etc.
Source: *Social Trends 29*, 1999 Edition, Eds Jil Matheson and John Pullinger, Office for National Statistics, London, The Stationery Office, 1999

Discuss

- Were there surprises in these statistics for you?
- How do we know how rich or poor we are? With whom do we usually compare ourselves?
- Does this work remind you of any passages in the Bible, either searching, challenging, or comforting?

Moneybox

In 1820 the richest 20 per cent of the world's population received 3 times as much as the poorest 20 per cent...

1870	7 times
1913	11 times
1960	30 times
1990	60 times
1997	74 times
1998	86 times

1999 United Nations Human Development Report, Oxford University Press, p3

Bible reading (5 minutes)
Invite someone to read James 2:1-7.

Discussion (20 minutes)
- Identify, from your own experience or observation, situations today in which the rich are treated with special consideration.
- Why is discrimination a matter of faith? James offers several reasons in the text – can you find them?

Voices from an unequal world (10 minutes)
James was passionately concerned about inequality. We continue by hearing what inequality means today.

Invite four people to read the following quotations from around the world.

Reader 1 From Uganda a community leader observes: 'The poorest families in this community cannot afford more than one meal a day, much less pay for medical treatment, clothe themselves, buy bedding, meet school fees, or taxes.'

Reader 2 From north London a single mother on low income says: 'We are denied choices, always buying the cheapest clothes and shoes, usually second-hand. Parents give the most nutritious food to their children and eat bread, margarine, leftovers – some don't eat much at all. Both obesity and malnutrition are common in mothers on low incomes. We can't choose how to use our leisure time because we can't afford the cost of public transport to reach even those facilities that are free to us. A seat at the opera can cost more than a week's benefit, so forget that. We have no choice but to accept even low paid and exploitative work or else lose benefits. A worker I know does 48 hours a week, but he still needs top up benefits to bring his family up to income support levels.'

Reader 3 From a factory in Asia, a mother of three says, 'I feel broken. I can't go on with this. My hands hurt, my body is worn out. I am always tired. God, where are you? Are you on TV? Are you in the supermarket? Are you on the assembly line?

Reader 4 From Perth, Scotland, a young single man says, 'Poverty equals lack of choice, lack of dignity, lack of access to power, being isolated, inequality. It is not just the poor affected by poverty. Poverty affects the whole society from the very top to the very bottom.'

British sources are quoted from testimonies published by Church Action on Poverty, Central Buildings, Oldham Street, Manchester M1 1JT. Website: www.church-poverty.org.uk
Asian and Ugandan quotes are from Christian Aid files.

Discuss

- How, in your own experience, do you feel 'poverty affects the whole society, from top to bottom?'

You have heard four modern voices and a Bible text.
- How, if at all, do the modern voices throw light on the Bible text?
- How, if at all, does the Bible text help to understand the modern voices?

Respond **Reflection and closing prayers** (20 minutes)
- As we think about the work that we have done together in this session, has there been any insight that you found challenging?
- Has there been an insight you felt is good news?
- What does the session leave you wanting to pray?

Invite comments. Explain that you will start with a time for silent or spoken prayers, then continue with prayers as they are written below.

Leader We pray in silence and aloud, with our words and what we feel.

Silent and spoken prayers are invited here.

Leader Jesus taught us to bring all our feelings and hopes together in prayer. We pray together as he taught us:

Our Father...

Invite two people to read the following prayers.

Leader When the world could not wait any longer, Jesus came and said:

Reader 1 The Spirit of the Lord is upon me, because he has anointed me to bring good news to the poor. He has sent me to proclaim release to the captives and recovery of sight to the blind, to let the oppressed go free to proclaim the year of the Lord's favour.

Luke 4:16-19

Moneybox

Lord, you come to us in neighbours we do not know and are unlikely to meet. You come to us when people's needs are measured in statistics, argued about in political programmes, or estimated in development plans. Help us to seek you in our best efforts at organisation, planning and thought, and so to love you with all our mind, strength and skill.

Anonymous

39

Leader   From assembly lines and fields of Asia, women
announce the good news:

Reader 2   In the midst of hunger and war
we celebrate the promise of plenty and peace.
In the midst of doubt and despair
we celebrate the promise of faith and hope.
In the midst of sin and decay
we celebrate the promise of salvation and renewal.
In the midst of death on every side
we celebrate the promise of the living Christ.

Asian Women Doing Theology, Singapore Conference Report, Nov 20-29 1987, Asian
Womens' Resource Centre for Culture and Theology, 566 Nattan Road, Kiu Kem Mansion 6/F,
Kowloon, Hong Kong

Leader   And we respond:

All   **O God, you promise a world**
where those who now weep shall laugh;
those who are hungry shall feast;
those who are poor now, and excluded,
shall have your kingdom for their own.
I want this world too.
I renounce despair.
I will act for change.
I choose to be included in your great feast of life.
Amen.

Janet Morley

Pass out the credit card-sized pieces of card. Invite the group
members to write a brief word or phrase that sums up the
way they have been thinking during the session. It may help to
write the headings 'Good news' and 'Challenge' on the cards
with spaces for the short phrases. The cards are to be put back
into their wallets or purses, as a way of reflecting an insight
in faith.

During the week

Reflect on the card on which you have written, and your wallet or purse, at least once. Use these as a starting point for prayer.

In preparation for an activity next week, read some national and local newspapers, and collect news clippings, pictures, stories, etc about money:
- the people who have it and don't have it
- community institutions that have it and don't have it
- relationships between people who have it and don't have it.

Moneybox
●●●●●●●●●●

For Africans, the idea of community still exists. In a community, people share in their sorrows and their happiness. The concerns of Christian Aid supporters are absolutely the right thing. For instance, when people grow tea or coffee, they need a place to sell. We depend on you and you depend on us. It is right for us to depend on each other. Get involved. We live together. This is part of your life too.

Thelli Ngaio, Coordinator, community based health-care programme, Church of the Province of Tanzania

Session 4 Giving

What kind of giving is good news?

Prepare   Bible texts: 2 Corinthians 8:1-15; Deuteronomy 14:22-26

In addition to a Bible and a copy of this book for each group member, for this session you will need:
- *a large sheet of paper*
- *a felt marker*
- *some recorded music to aid reflection (optional).*

To give a joyful focus to the closing reflections, consider and bring a gift for each member of the group. It should be something thoughtful but without much financial value (eg a leaf, a feather, a walnut, a scripture text, a flower, a fruit, a prayer card, a night light, a sprig of herbs, a joke, a piece of cake... use your imagination!) It need not be the same thing for each person. Turn to page 48 to find out how you will use this during the closing prayer.

Identify people in advance to prepare to read:
- *the opening and closing prayers*
- *the two Bible readings*
- *the story from Brazil.*

Gather   **Introduction** (10 minutes)
Repeat the exercise which helps the group to settle, relax and focus on God as described at the beginning of the first session.

At the end of last week's session it was suggested that everyone looked during the week for headlines and photographs which related to the theme. Everyone should have the opportunity to show the rest of the group what they have brought, and explain why it caught their eye.

Opening prayers (5 minutes)
Invite the group to say the prayer on the inside front cover.

In the silence, ask God what gift you would like to receive during the course of this session.

Keep silence

Moneybox

A pig and a hen were walking past a church. On a noticeboard, an accusing finger pointed at the passers-by, asking the question: 'What will you do for poor people?'

'I know what we could do,' clucked the hen to the pig. 'We could team up and lay on a bacon and egg supper to raise money.'

'It's all right for you to suggest that,' grumbled the pig. 'For you that would be a gift; for me it would be a sacrifice!'

Now take the opportunity to tell him what you feel able to give to him before the meeting comes to a close.

Keep silence for a short time then sing or say the following:

All   **What can I give him, poor as I am?**
If I were a shepherd I would give a lamb;
if I were a wise man I would do my part;
so what I have I give him,
give my heart.

Christina Rosetti

Discussion (10 minutes)

Starting with the leader, everyone should have a chance to tell the rest of the group about something that they have been given. It need not be anything remarkable, but mention something that sticks in the memory because it brought joy, or was a surprise, or marked a special event, or perhaps even because it was not wanted.

When everyone has had a chance to share that simple memory, invite the group to suggest a time when they have been given something that money could not buy.

This time the answers might refer to emotions, to people, to memories or something for which there is no one to thank except God.

• What motivates people to give presents? Which would you say are 'good' reasons? Which might be suspect?
• Is it ever difficult to receive a gift?

Reflect   Bible reading (10 minutes)

Try to think yourself into the circumstances under which Paul wrote the part of the Bible you are about to hear, some 25 years after Jesus' resurrection. One of the most widely travelled people of his day, he was pausing during one of his relentless journeys to write a letter. He was many miles from Jerusalem, where the first church had been founded, but his thoughts were constantly with the Christians there. They had not long recovered from a famine throughout the whole region which had brought appalling misery. Everyone had suffered, but the Christian community was suffering more than most. Because they had converted from Judaism to Christianity they were in disgrace with their families, had been cut off from contact with them, and had lost their jobs. Without money or food, their situation was desperate.

Paul was lodging in Macedonia, an area that had itself been battered by a series of civil wars in which the Christians had been persecuted and reduced to poverty. The letter he was writing was addressed to a church in Corinth which was thriving and substantially more wealthy than the town in which he was staying. His colleague Titus had gone ahead to inform the Corinthian church of what was happening in Jerusalem, and this was not the first time Paul had written to them, so there was no excuse for the Christians to plead ignorance of the needs back in Jerusalem.

Before we hear the Bible passage, guess what you think Paul would have said to those people about giving. Make a list of things that you would say if you had been him! The leader should write down the suggestions that emerge.

Invite someone to read 2 Corinthians 8:1-15.

Discussion (20 minutes)

• Go through the list you made and see whether the guesses you made actually appeared in the passage.
• What other instructions did Paul give that you can now add to the list?
• One of the surprises of the passage is that Paul suggests that those who give generously find that they are receiving more than they are giving. In what ways might that be true? (He writes more about this in 2 Corinthians 9:6-15.)
• What kinds of 'dramatic change' would we need to make if we took this Bible passage seriously? What stops us making those changes? What could help us make them?

A story from Brazil (15 minutes)

Turn to the colour photographs in the centre of the book. Among them you will find a picture of workers in the plantations of Bahia, Brazil. You are about to hear the story of a writer who went to the plantation so that he could give an account of the lives of those who earned a living there. However, he was given something he could never have expected.

Invite someone to read this story.

Reader After a journey across three continents over a period of almost a year, the demand of poor communities for justice reverberated most powerfully for me in the words of a woman I could not name. Maria, I had called her, because she was too frightened to give her real name, supposing that if her identity was known she would lose her job as a cocoa harvester on the plantation of Fazenda Agua Branca outside the town of Wenceslau Guimares in the middle of Bahia, Brazil.

We had met deep in the forest of cocoa trees. She had thought I was a buyer from one of the multinational cocoa-processing firms that set the terms under which she worked.

'Raise the minimum wage,' she had said. 'We work hard here, but we do not get enough to live off. We get some wage rises, but the price rises are always more and faster. I have nine small children to feed. They are not getting enough to eat. My husband is ill and cannot work. I cannot afford the medicine for him. We work hard, but we do not get enough to live.'

Maria was not asking for charity. She was not asking for aid. She was asking for a fair wage for her back-breaking day's work. She was asking for justice.

I had thought our conversation was over, for it seemed there was nothing left to say. The canopy of leaves above me suddenly felt oppressive and I walked on through the forest of cocoa trees until I came upon a clearing bathed in a shaft of sunlight. The air felt fresher there and the waxy leaves of the cocoa trees shone in the bright sunlight as if they had been polished.

There was a cough behind me. It was Maria. She stood for a moment in the pool of light. Her tattered shirt, which had

Moneybox
●●●●●●●●●●●

In Leviticus 25, the land belongs to God. The ten per cent of tithing is symbolic of the 100 per cent that belongs to God. We are almost at the point now where the richest have 100 times what the poor have.

Ross Kinsler, US Presbyterian Bible scholar, based in Costa Rica (see Moneybox on page 38)

45

looked dirty and dingy in the gloom of the undergrowth, now looked brilliantly colourful, and the yellow cocoa pods in the large basket slung from her shoulder glinted like gold in the sunshine. She smiled, for the first time, and produced from behind her a small bundle, wrapped in an old cloth.

'You have come far into the plantation with no food,' she said. 'It's lunchtime.' Swinging the basket down to the ground she squatted on a fallen tree and untied the corners of the cloth. Inside was a ball of sticky yellow-white porridge. 'It is farofa, cassava flour mixed with palm oil,' she said, and began to chat to cover my silence. 'There are no beans or meat, I am afraid. Cold beans are bad for the digestion; they bring stomach ache. And meat, I am sorry, but we hardly talk about meat these days. But the farofa is good. Come eat. It is good to share.'

I looked at the small mound of food. Embarrassed, I began to mutter that I was not hungry.

'Nonsense,' she replied. 'It is a long way back to the town. I have food; you have none. It is my duty to share with you.' She pulled a lump from the yellowy ball and held it out to me.

Paul Vallely, from *Promised Lands*, Fount/Christian Aid, 1992

Moneybox

God wants to give us something, but he cannot because our hands are full – there's nowhere for him to put it.

St Augustine of Hippo, 4th century African bishop

In pairs, talk about the following questions.
• What is your reaction to this story about a meeting between two people of such unequal means?
• What do you imagine happened immediately after the part of the story you have heard? What do you suppose Paul and Maria went away thinking?
• Obviously, there are ways in which giving is costly. Are there ways in which giving sets us free?

Respond   **Planning a response** (15 minutes)
Invite someone to read Deuteronomy 14:22-26.

• In some ways the 'tithe' offering which was made by the Hebrews was of no practical use to others – it simply served to bring honour to God and joy to the givers. What would these people have lost had they not been generous enough to make this gift to God?
• What can we learn from the Old Testament practice of tithing? Obviously the life and teaching of Jesus has set Christians free from obeying the strict laws of the Hebrews.

Does that mean that tithing has no relevance to today's lifestyle?

- The practical business of Christian giving raises endless dilemmas – for example, there will always be competing demands from the world's poorest communities and the leak in the church roof! Do members of the group have any experience of deciding how much and to whom to give which would be helpful to share with the others?

During the week ahead, think about whether the group could take some action together as a response to what you have been talking about during this session. Write some thoughts about what you might like to do in the space below. Come next week ready to tell the others what you have been thinking.

Closing prayers (5 minutes)

Invite the group to sit with their hands cupped open in their laps and their eyes closed. Suggest that, during a minute or two of silence, everyone in the group should use their imagination. They are to think about the three different gifts suggested below, some real, some imaginary, and picture them being placed in their hands.

- First of all, everyone is to imagine that they are standing in a clearing in the cocoa plantations of Bahia, Brazil. Feel the heat and the humidity. Smell the rich forest air. From behind a tree Maria comes toward you, lunch in hand. Will you share her lunch? Will you share her quest for just conditions?
- Next, think about something in the past that you are glad you have been given. Now as you feel it, as it were in your hands, comes a chance to thank God for what it means to you.
- Finally – and it may take a vivid imagination to picture this being placed in your hands – consider something which God has given you.

Either hold a time of open prayer during which members of the group thank God for any or all of these things, or simply talk to each other about your gratitude for these things knowing that God is unseen but present at the conversation. Close this time of prayer or conversation by reverting to closed eyes and open hands. While this is happening, place in each hand a gift to take away as a joyful reminder of what has happened during this session (see the section headed 'Prepare' at the beginning of this chapter for more details).

Invite someone to read these words, which are by Helder Camara, who was for many years Archbishop of Recife, Brazil.

Reader

Almighty God,
may your bounty teach me greatness of heart;
may your magnificence stop me being mean;
seeing you a prodigal and open-handed giver,
let me give unstintingly like a king's son,
like God's own.

Close your prayers by saying the Lord's Prayer together (the words in full are on page 19).

Our Father...

Moneybox

●●●●●●●●●●●

Once upon a time there was a prince who lived in a grand castle. Every day he would leave his castle in a splendid carriage to visit the daughter of the duchess in her palace. One day, by the beautiful gate of the castle, he noticed what looked like a tattered heap of rags squatting miserably. 'That poor beggar,' he thought to himself. He opened the window of the carriage and tossed a coin out so that it landed just at the foot of the bundle.

The next day he saw the dismal sight again. Once again he threw a coin from his window and hurried by. This grew into a habit each day, and the prince thought less and less about what he was doing. It didn't cost him much, after all!

Then one morning, he got held up by a particularly annoying courtier. He was in such a rush that he told the coach driver: 'Fast as you can! Go, go, go!' The driver lurched off at speed, cutting all the corners in the courtyard and scattering the servants. He sped through the gate so fast that the carriage was on two wheels and, splat, it crashed straight into the heap of rags and sent it flying...

It was not a beggar; it was a crate of rotting bananas.

Session 5 **Wanting**

How do we make sense of all the things we desire?

Prepare Bible texts: 1 Timothy 6:6-19; Matthew 13:44-48

In addition to a Bible and a copy of this book for each group member, for this session you will need:
• cards with items to be 'auctioned' written on – see page 51 – write the words in the table opposite on ten separate cards
• a pencil or pen for everyone
• recorded music to aid reflection (optional).

Identify people in advance to prepare to read:
• the opening and closing prayers
• the two Bible readings.

Gather Introduction (10 minutes)
Repeat the exercise which helps the group to settle, relax and focus on God as described at the beginning of the first session.

At the end of last week's session it was suggested that members of the group considered individually during the week whether a joint action in response to last week's discussions about giving might be appropriate. Invite them to comment on what they have been thinking during the week. Are there suggestions to follow up? Plans to make?

Opening prayers (10 minutes)
Invite the group to say the prayer on the inside front cover.

Invite the group to turn to the centre page in their books, where the cover image is shown as a poster. Invite them to dwell on it in silence for a little while. With a few seconds to think about each statement, read out the following words to guide their thoughts.

Leader Here, on a market stall in Ireland, is a selection of goods. Throughout the course you will have seen this image. What thoughts does it bring to your mind now as we come to the end of this course?
• Is Jesus out of place in this picture, or where he belongs?
• In what ways, or not, is Jesus a choice to be made?
• Is Jesus on offer here for love or money?

Read the following words as the group looks at the picture.

Leader The Kingdom of Heaven is like a merchant looking for fine pearls. When he found one of great value, he went away and sold everything he had and bought it.

Sing the song on page 13 or play a piece of reflective music (optional).

Reflect **Life auction** (20 minutes)
Place the ten cards to be auctioned in the middle of the group.

Lasting good health	£
Close and supportive family life	£
Creative, artistic or musical talent	£
Warm and happy friendships	£
Physical beauty	£
Active sporting life	£
Worry-free financial comfort	£
Career full of achievement	£
Adventure and excitement	£
Respect for who you are and what you do	£
Total	**£100**

How much do you want those things? You are going to attend an auction at which you can 'bid' for them! Imagine you have £100 to spend. You have three minutes to divide up your £100 between the ten things – but only the person who bids most for each one will get it! You can allocate all the money to one and nothing to the other nine, or give £10 to each, or any variation in between – it all depends how much you want that item for yourself.

First of all, decide how much you will allocate to each thing and write it in the table. At this stage, keep it secret from the rest of the group. Make sure that the total doesn't exceed £100.

After three minutes, the leader will hold up each card in turn and everyone can say how much they bid for it. The card goes to the person who bid the most. If there is a draw, have half each!

At the end, take stock of who has ended up with what.
- Are you surprised at what you ended up with?
- Is there anything you really wanted which has gone to someone else?
- What other items could have been included on the list?
- Does this exercise remind you of any stories or passages in the Bible?

Bible reading (5 minutes)
Invite someone to read 1 Timothy 6:6-19.

Discussion (15 minutes)
- Look through the passage, imagining yourself to be rich. Which phrases would give you:
  - an encouragement?
  - a warning?
  - an idea that might change your way of living?
- Look through the passage again, imagining yourself to be poor. Which phrases would give you:
  - an encouragement?
  - a warning?
  - an idea that might change your way of living?
- Having said that wanting money can lead to all kinds of evil, Paul suggests six alternative things to set our hearts on (verse 11). Why do you think he picked those? What others could he have added to the list? Why do you suppose he described faith as 'a fight'?

Life that is truly life (20 minutes)
Invite someone to read Matthew 13:44-48.

Leader   Quickly, without too much thought, based on these word pictures, call out words that describe what the Kingdom of Heaven is like. What does it cost? What is it worth?

For this activity, turn to the person sitting next to you and work in pairs.

Pick one of the three images: the treasure in a field; the man in search of a pearl; or the net. Think back on all you have discussed about faith and money, and discuss: if you were

Moneybox

Take, Lord, and receive all my liberty, my memory, my understanding, and my entire will – all that I have and possess. Thou hast given it all to me. To thee, O Lord, I return it. All is thine! Dispose of it wholly according to thy will. Give me thy love and thy grace, for this is sufficient for me.

Ignatius of Loyola, founder of the Jesuit order, 1491-1566

writing a parable today in contemporary language, to have the same impact as these three which Jesus told, what modern-day setting would you choose? (Here is an example: perhaps the Kingdom of Heaven is like discovering on *The Antiques Roadshow* that among all the cheap imitations you have collected you have come into possession of a unique original.)

Write your idea down to use in the final prayers.

Moneybox

To know what kind of God you believe in, I have to know what idols you fight. It is a trick that Europe wants to play on the rest of the world to say that there are no idols any more. But there is the idol of accumulating wealth... Idols present themselves as true Gods; like the divinity, they feel they need no justification.

Jon Sobrino, Jesuit priest, El Salvador

Session 5 **Wanting**

Form yourselves into a group again to discuss the following question.

Look back on the goals of the course which were described at the end of the introduction. Have the activities of the last five weeks helped you to:

- share insights in faith?
- consider how faith can change the way you get, spend, own, give, want?
- reflect on how money can change the way you worship and pray?

Respond **Closing prayers** (10 minutes)

Close your prayers by saying the Lord's Prayer together (the words in full are on page 19).

Our Father...

Leader We remember that Jesus taught that the Kingdom of Heaven is like:
a treasure hidden in a field,
a merchant in search of pearls,
a net that gathers of every kind.
And also the Kingdom of Heaven is like...

At this point invite people to read their descriptions.

Leader We remember what the Kingdom of Heaven costs.
We remember what the Kingdom of Heaven is worth.
And in the silence we examine ourselves to ask, as Easter approaches:
what do we truly want?

Keep silence

Moneybox

When shall these longings be sufficed that stir my spirit night and day?
When shall I see my country lay her homage at the feet of Christ?
Of all I have, O Saviour sweet,
all gifts, all skill, all thoughts of mine,
a living garland I entwine,
and offer at thy lotus feet.

Narayam Vaman Tilak, Indian poet and hymn-writer, 1900

Invite someone to read the following prayer.

Reader I want my eyes opened to the reality of other people,
to hear what they are not able to articulate...
I want to see justice run like a river,
bringing healing and peace to the nations...
I want the eyes of my heart to see the grace of God
that is present in every child, woman and man I meet.
I want to be able
to see differently, to think differently, to live kindly,
to walk humbly, to serve graciously and gratefully.
Come, Lord Jesus!

All **Come always and save me –
that I may want what you want,
that I may live in you,
that I may be completely holy.**

Romeo L del Rosario, Malaysia

About Christian Aid

We believe in life before death

As the sponsored agency of 40 churches in the UK and Ireland, Christian Aid works in around 60 countries to alleviate poverty and fight the causes of poverty. This means:

- giving emergency aid when required;
- funding local projects that bring about long-term benefits for poor people – in health, agriculture and urban community groups, projects that provide low cost credit and generate income, or that lobby for improvements in rural working conditions. In the UK, Christian Aid funds organisations like the Fairtrade Foundation which promotes fair terms of trade, better prices and decent working conditions for people who produce the goods we buy;
- listening to those people about the causes of their poverty and arguing their case to those who have the power to change things.

Trade for life

We want to change the rules that keep people poor, such as international trade rules that reduce the price of things poor people produce, and make them even more vulnerable to the power of global capital.

The British government has signed up to targets set by the United Nations to halve the proportion of people in poverty by the year 2015. This goal is ambitious. To achieve it, Christian Aid is pressing for big changes.

- **In global trade rules:** The rules that work against the interests of poor people must be stopped. But that's not all. We have to work for new rules that help wipe out poverty rather than making it worse.
- **For transnational corporations:** New regulations are needed to channel some of the enormous power and influence of transnational corporations to help eradicate poverty.
- **In our own personal choices:** People with enough wealth have a choice about whether and how to use their influence in ways to help eradicate poverty. The choice is ours, particularly in the use of our personal wealth. We can also influence the institutions in which we take part – as shareholders, church members, staff in pension plans, consumers, etc.

For Love or Money was written because we believe that at the heart of the Gospel is an invitation – and challenge – to engage with these issues. If you agree, tick the areas you would like to explore further on the response form attached to the cover.